How to build a business from scratch backwards and start making money in less than 30days

I want you to imagine just for a minute sitting in your home in the morning, drinking your favorite beverage, looking out your back patio at a beautiful blue sky and thinking how great life is. You don't have any worries, no problems, and you are so happy that your started the business of your dreams just 12 months ago.

This is a dream for many people. Many people still dream this today, but there is no end in site. The debts keep piling up, the collectors are calling each day and they are just begging for a way to get out of the "hell-hole" they are in.

We have come to the conclusion that the government is a joke, the stock market is for whom ever is stupid enough to play it and it is only a matter of time that you lose your job because there is no such thing as a "safe job."

So at the end of the day, what are you going to do? Are you going to keep playing the same game you have been playing or are you going to change your game plan and do something for yourself.

Are you going to seize the moment, use this workbook and start creating your own future today?

If you are ready to make some changes and start living the life you have always dreamed of then you better get out a pencil or pen and start going through this workbook.

Or

If I am just wasting your time, just put the workbook down now or at least have the decentsy to give it to someone else that it having the same dreams or a great life as you.

Why did I make a workbook and not a book?

I do a lot of reading every day. Reading is good. It is something that everyone should do every day. There are 100's of great books out there.

Here's the thing. Are you one of those that needs to make some money NOW or

- Do you want to wait several months or years to read what you're supposed to do
- Then try to figure out what you just read
- Then try to make a go of it.

Unfortunately, in this trying economy we don't have time to do that.

If you have the time to do that this is probably not for you. This workbook allows you to start creating successes in starting your own business today.

This workbook will give you step by step instructions and activities of what to do and how to do it. There is no reading and then trying to figure out what you just read. Just follow the simple instructions and do the activity specified in each step.

When I was putting together this workbook, I asked myself why do people start businesses?

- Job loss
- need more money
- financial hardship
- cannot get a job
- want to get out of the rat race
- financial freedom

The list goes on and on.

I think most people believe that starting a business is going to be a "piece of cake."

I will let you know right now that it takes a lot of work to create a successful business. If you have the desire to do whatever it takes <u>you will succeed</u>.

If followed, this workbook is set up to help you start making money within 30days. It will take you through all the steps needed:

- How to create a real product or service
- How to make the money you need to succeed
- How to help you understand all the things that most small businesses will never know

Many people ask me?

What is so special about your workbook? There many books and systems out there that can help start a business.

There are several reasons that this workbook is the most superior business start-up guide out there.

1. This is the only workbook that you don't need a dictionary to figure out what the author is saying
2. This is the only workbook that you can actually write in, make notes and after completing one step you can feel like you accomplished something to get you closer to starting your business
3. This is the only workbook that will help you to understand all the work it takes to start a business. Lets face it. Many people want to start a business but really don't want to start a business, they want a hobby.

4. This is the only workbook that will take you by the hand and guide you through the steps to starting a real business. I am not teaching you how to start a new hobby. Most business start-up books give you ideas and suggestions. You don't need suggestions; you need to know exactly what to do to start a business.
5. This is the only workbook that will not only help you in your business, but you will find that many of the steps can help you in life's pursuits.

In this workbook, you will learn step by step to

- Find something you love to do
- Market that idea
- Sell it
- And Make Money

Many people ask me who am I, what's my story?

I was born in New York City to awesome, but poor parents. When I was just a young kid, I always knew that there was something bigger than me and I just had to find it. So, self employment seemed to be the way to look for it. Like most self employed, or what I call entrepreneurs, I always had great ideas. I always struggled to find how to make myself successful. I was fortunate enough to make my first million dollars at age 30. I also found out what it's like to lose a million dollars. I have had many failed businesses and have learned the hard way. I have taken many risks that no normal person would ever imagine taking. I have had so many business failures it makes my head spin to even think about them all. But I have also hit many big opportunities out of the ball park and had many huge successes.

The reality is I'm still alive to talk about it and I make a very comfortable living today with my wife and four boys.

So, the point is, do you want to learn from someone that has made so many failures in his life and still lives to talk about it?

I would hope you say YES,

Because the contents in this workbook will tell you exactly what to do right and not make all the mistakes I made.

I am going to take out

- all the STOPS
- all the Nonsense
- and ALL the ridiculous vocabulary words that don't make any sense to over 80% of the world

6

and help you to start making MONEY in 30 days.

I am going to teach you stuff that most businesses owners would die to know.

In this workbook, I promise to::

- **Keep it Real • Keep it True • and No B.S.** (sorry I cannot spell it out)

Jump on for the ride and LETS MAKE SOME MONEY.

Yours Truly,

Eric "the Business Makin Machine" Erickson

How to use this workbook

Each step will take you through an exercise. Follow the exercise. As you complete each exercise you will be putting together various things you need to run a successful small business. Think of it like putting together a puzzle.

Don't be afraid to write in this workbook, it is a workbook.

Make notes, doodle, and write whatever you need to help you remember things you want to. There is plenty of room to write.

These steps are designed to help you be imaginative, creative and increase creativity

As you are doing a step, an idea may pop into your head. Write it down. We will take all those ideas and use them later.

You can go through these steps as slow or as fast as you want.

It is recommended that you take a 15-30 minute break between steps to help calm your mind so you can refocus on the next step. So go get a drink of water or step outside in the fresh air.

IMPORTANT – make sure all distractions are eliminated. Turn off the cellular phone, phone, and don't check email. This will help you to stay focused and make sure the creative juices flowing.

Each step takes anywhere from 30-90 min... depending upon how much info you have to write down.

There will be some steps that you will have a hard time with… don't worry, you can go back to that step later. Sometimes completing another step will help you to complete the one you are having trouble with.

Most importantly, RELAX and have FUN.

This will be the easiest workbook you have ever used.

STEP ONE

READY TO BUILD A BUSINESS?

I am going to teach you how to build a business BACKWARDS!

YES, Backwards!

Many people come up with the idea, product or service first and then move onto advertising and making a business. They forget the most important things first.

STOP!

NOTE: I need to get something out of the way before we get started. This is REALLY important.

READ CAREFULLY!

I am going to sound greedy for a moment

Don't be alarmed

You will understand once you complete the first step

Reality Check: What you are about to do is **ALL about the MONEY**

Don't **EVER** let anyone tell you different

You are starting a business to make **GREENBACKS…MONEY!**

There is no need to be ashamed or embarrassed.

WOW! I feel much better now.

So the first step in putting together your business is to identify how much money you need to make so your business a success.

YES you need to pay yourself… You don't want to go hungry trying to make your dream come true.

Most businesses go bad and get thrown off the Empire State Building because they can afford to stay in business.

So, we are going to create budget if you will. This is not a traditional budget, this will help you to know what you have, what you are responsible for paying and how much your business needs to make to help you accomplish you goal of not being poor anymore.

First I want you to list all the all your things you own: car, house, boats, etc

What you Own	What you Owe (how much)	What's it worth (how much)
1.		
2.		
3.		
4.		
5.		
6.		
7.		

NOTE: YES, There will be some duplication.

Now write down who you owe, write down payment and balance

Who you owe payment (monthly) balance

Who do you owe	Monthly payment	Balance
1.	$	$
2.	$	$
3.	$	$
4.	$	$
5.	$	$
6.	$	$
7.	$	$

If you need more room, you can keep going…

8.	$	$
9.	$	$
10.	$	$
11.	$	$
12.	$	$
13.	$	$
14.	$	$
15.	$	$

Add up the total monthly amount and put it below. If you want to know how much your balance is you can do that to.

TOTALS	$	$

Now I want you to write down what you have liquid. That means if you had to leave town today and could not sell the house, cars, boats, etc. How much cash, gold etc do you have that you would take with you.

Bank Account(s)	$
Saving(s)	$
Gold, Silver, Jewelry, etc	$
Cash that you hide in the house	$

Now we are going to write down your budget

Who do you pay each month?	How much do you pay them?
House, apartment, condo, etc	$
Car, Truck, transportation	$
Gas for your transportation	$
Food	$
Credit cards (Add all monthly fees for all)	$
Insurances (health, auto, medical, etc)	$
Entertainment	$

Have more to write down, put it below. You want to know everything you spend each month.

	$
	$
	$
	$
	$
TOTAL you spend each month (B)	$

Now we are going to write down how much you are currently bringing home each month. This is not gross, this is net, (how much you put into your hands to spend each month). This also includes alimony money or any other sources you get money from others. (Please don't include any illegal money, that's a bad way to start). Sorry, a little humor.

$ _____ (A)

Now subtract how much you bring home each month from how much you pay out each month.

Money you bring home each month $_____ (A)

Money you spend each month $_____ (B)

Subtract "A" from "B". TOTAL $ _____

Is it negative or positive? _____

If you have any extra money left over how much is it? $_____

Now write down how much money you want to make each month with your new business.

$ _____ (write it in BIG NUMBERS)

If you are looking to supplement your income or if you do not want to quit your job and just make a little extra write down what that amount is.

IF you are done working for someone else, write down how much money you need to make each month.

So why did we just do this? Now you know how much money it takes to run your life each day.

So if your business is such that you need to quit what you are currently doing you now know how much money you need to make to keep you standard of living.

Example: Let's say your total monthly bills equal $2,465 per month. You want to make $2,465 per month or better each month.

Hold on to this number, We will use this step later.

Now take a break, get a drink of water and I will see you in the next step.

STEP TWO

Brain Storming Session: Many people usually start a business because they are good at something.

They usually have a hobby or a job they do at home or work they can make money with it.

I am going to take you through an exercise that will help you to identify all that you are good at. This may be talents, hobbies, if you have been doing something at work you are really good at.

You are going to write down all the things you are good at

Below write down all your talents, hobbies, specifically what you do for work (this maybe several different things). If you start telling yourself that you don't have any talents or things your good at I am going to reach through this book and hit you over the head.

So don't be ashamed or embarrassed or shy. This is the time to say, "I AM GOOD AT……"

_____

_____

_____

_____

_____

_____

_____

_____

_____

_____

_____

_____

_____

_____

_____

_____

_____

_____

_____

NOTES, THOUGHTS, DOODLES

Now that you have a long list of all the things you are good at.

You need to see which of these things that you are good at that can make you money.

Remember how I mentioned before. This is about the MONEY.

More importantly making you the money that you said you needed to make to keep your current standard of living or better.

So which of these ideas are going to make you the money you need? This is where we need to do a little research.

The easiest way to do this is get on the internet at home, work or at the library, go to your favorite search website (google, yahoo, bing, etc) and search the things you are good at.

What are you going to search?

You are looking to see if others have a business doing what you are good at.

Example: Lets say I love to cook brownies. I would go to google, yahoo, bing, etc and search homemade brownies and see if anyone has a business selling homemade brownies. You are going to make some simple notes that include how many businesses you found selling homemade brownies and how much they are selling a brownie for.

Another example: Lets say I am a plumber for a living. I'm thinking about starting my own plumbing business. I would go to google, yahoo, bing, etc and type in plumbers in your area and maybe go to their websites and see what they charge.

Get the idea?

NOTE: There may be certain things you are going to research that may be hard to find on the internet so you may need to call people in your area and see what they are charging. Act like you are a person wanting to buy their product or service. In some cases you may need to go to a store front to find the information you need.

Is this a lot of work…

> **YES.. but I cannot tell you how important it is to do this. About 90% of small businesses never do this and about 80% of them fail in their business in the first year.**

Take your time doing this step.

Don't rush! If you are seeing common themes or idea write them down.

The best ideas come from researching the things you already know how to do.

NOTE: many of my customers always ask what the purpose of this activity is. The most important reason for this activity is you need to find an opportunity that you enjoy and you can make the money you need as we discussed in the first step.

Example: let's say you decided to you want to sell homemade brownies and you found that the average sell price of a brownie is $1.00. You decided in step 1 that you want to make $5,000 per month… that's 5,000 brownies per month… that's a lot of brownies… are you willing to make 5000 brownies per month…maybe not.

 RESEARCH AREA (write down what you have found out below. (The next page will also help you to ask the right questions and give you some places to search for your ideas. Write down the information that is important.)

_____

_____

_____

_____

_____

_____

_____

_____

_____

_____

_____

_____

_____

_____

NOTES, THOUGHTS, DOODLES

Research Area (CONTINUED)

What is the Idea?

What product or services are being offered?

What are the prices they are selling for?

What else is interesting about the business you called that you might be interested in?

****** Write down the other places on the net they can go to research**********

Some good places to go are Amazon.com, ebay.com and dummies.com

What did you find? What business do you want to create?

STEP THREE

Now you have an idea of products/services you can offer; now it's time to write down who you know.

Many people always have great ideas and then when it comes time to advertise and market their product they forget to tell the great news to the people they know. Why spend money on marketing and advertising to people you don't know when you can market your product for free to people you know.

So below, on the left, you will see a prospect building chart. This will help you to get the juices flowing and help you remember the people that you know. For right now only write down names, you can worry about the phone numbers and contact info later.

Who Do You Know?　　　　　　　　　　_____

Family Members　　　　　　　　　　　_____

Extended family like Aunts/Uncles/Cousins　_____

Brothers/Sisters　　　　　　　　　　_____

Church members　　　　　　　　　　_____

Hairdresser/Barber　　　　　　　　　_____

Grocery Store　　　　　　　　　　　_____

Local hang out (bar, night club, VFW)　　_____

25

Where do you go to give service?   _____

Civic clubs – Rotary, Kiwanis   _____

Who are the companies that sold your home?   _____

Who do you contact and talk to each day?   _____

Your kids parents   _____

Parent Teacher Associations (PTA)   _____

Who is on your facebook, twitter and linked in?   _____

Who do you talk to at your kids sport activities?   _____

What stores do you go to buy stuff?   _____

Moms groups   _____

_____

_____

_____

_____

_____

_____

_____

START WRITING NAMES! We are not focusing on addresses, phone # and email addresses, just names. Once you have written down all the names you can go back and fill in contact info.

NOTES, THOUGHTS, DOODLES

STOP!

Take a break and remember everything we have done so far

CHECKLIST – Have you completed all these steps?

- ☐ Budget
- ☐ List of what your good at
- ☐ Research – what product/service is going to make you money
- ☐ Who do you know list

What have you learned so far?

Any comments you want to write down so you can remember later?

Great Job!

STEP FOUR

When we make a decision and figure out what we really want it is important to bring all the previous steps that we have worked thus far together and use them to see what it is we really want.

I have been fortunate in my life to know many multi millionaires. One particular millionaire taught me an amazing lesson.

This lesson is in the form of a game. The game is really easy but will have significant value to you when you finish it.

Below there are numbers 1-11. I want you to think of the things that are important to you. Be very specific and detailed.

What should you put on each line? You can put in goals you have, dreams or desires you have. Maybe you want to pay off your house or be debt free. Or maybe it is to be successful in your business in a certain period of time or have a better relationship with your significant other.

Write them down and remember to be very detailed. I want you to write down either 7 or 11 items. It needs to be 7 or 11items…. This is very important.

The objective of the game is to figure out which of these items is the most important. How are you going to do that? You are going to match them up with each other and the one that is more important you are going to put a tally mark to the left of that item #.

Example: in order to make the game be successful, you are going to start with number 1 and match it with 2 and put a tally mark to the left of the item number that is more important.

Example: Say you wrote down to be debt free in 2yrs on item 1 and on number 2 you wrote to go on one date with your significant other per week. You decided that having a date at least weekly was more important so you put a tally mark to the left of item 2.

No w you will continue this: match 1 and 2, 1 and 3, 1 and 4....3 and 4, 3 and 5, 3 and 6....6 and 7

Add up the tally marks and see which item has the most tally marks.

Tally	Description

Write the item that you choose below.

Now write some thoughts down as to why you think you chose this item.

Don't think about it, just write…

NOTES, THOUGHTS, DOODLES

Now, I want you to match up some of the ideas for a business that you researched and match that up with the item that you identified you want.

Are there any similarities between what business you chose to start and what you thought what most important to you?

Maybe this exercise has made you think about a different business you need to start?

Maybe this exercise has made it clear to you that you should not start a business?

Write down your thoughts.

IMPORTANT NOTE: Pay particular attention to the ideas that will help you get what you want.

NOTE: many people ask, what about the other items that I wanted. They are important to me also.

Answer: So there is a belief that says if you do what you really want to do the rest will come.

So, don't worry about the other items that you want. Once you make your plan to get what you want, the rest will come.

SNAP SHOT: Start Putting it Together

Below write down some notes of what type of business you want to start.

Keep in mind step 1 that tells you how much money you need to make.

The business you select should give you the money you need to make and fulfill the item that had the most tally marks.

Write down:

Type of Business I am going to start:

Who am I going to sell it to? Who is my target audience?

What price(s) am I going to charge?

How am I going to use all the people I know to market my business for FREE?

How much extra money do I have each month to use for my business? (use step 1)

NOTES, THOUGHTS, DOODLES

CONGRATS!

Hopefully you have found the type of business you want to start.

We are not done yet.

So let's move on to the "how are we going to get this done"

STEP FIVE

The Business Plan

You have figured out:

- ☐ How much money you want to make
- ☐ What type of business you want to start
- ☐ You have figured out what is most important to you

Now let me show you how to put it all together and put together a simple business plan so you can stay focused.

Why are we going to write a business plan?

It is important to have a direction and having something written will help you to stay on the road to making money.

The business plan I am going to show you is what I call a free flowing plan. It is meant to be changed. So don't worry if it doesn't sound right… you can change it later.

Most business plans are written in paragraph form and when you are done you have written a book. We are not going to do that. This plan will be a bunch of notes and bullet points to help you stay on task.

So we are going to start by writing what we call an executive summary. An executive summary tells you what you are specifically going to do, how you are going to do it and what you need to be successful.

You have already written down some notes, so use those notes to answer the following questions.

Time to write:

1. Write down what exactly what you are going to do in your new company. Describe your company

2. Write down what exactly you are going to sell. Be very specific. If it's multiple items or services, write them all down.

3. Write down how you are going to sell your products or services. Example: Store, internet, flea market, etc

4. Write down what you need to accomplish this. Maybe you need a website, or a store front or a place to store your inventory. May be you need a small amount of money. Be very specific.

5. Write down why are you doing this business. What do you want to accomplish and what are your goals. These goals can be monetary or you may say you want to sell so many units or you want to help so many people. Use the step where you played the game. This step should help you identify and describe why you want to start this business.

Write down what is so special about what you want to do. What sets you apart from the others?

Explain the products in detail you want to sell. Break it down so you know who you buy the supplies from, how much they cost and what you are going to sell them for.

In this section you want to talk about your competition. Who are they? What do you do better than them? How are you going to compete against them?

Write down how you are going to marketing your products/services. Remember this is an ever changing document. If you are going to market using the newspaper, flyers, postcards, website, door to door selling. Social media. Write down these ideas.

In step one you decided how much you need to make each month with your business. When you sell your product or service unfortunately you don't get to keep all the money. You are going to have what called "cost of goods." This basically means that you are going to have a product or service that costs you money. This is the cost of the good. Now you need to mark that cost up so you can sell it for a profit

This is an easy thing to do. You will take your selling price and deduct your costs. Your costs are the price you bought the product for (cost of goods). Or if you have a service you need to tell yourself how much you charge yourself to work in the business. Do you need to include transportation costs or telephone costs?

Subtract your price you are selling your product or service for and deduct your total cost of goods and this is your net profit. Net profit is the money you make after paying all the items associated with selling that product or service. Now you take what you want to make per month and divide into you cost per product or service.

Example; if you are selling brownies and it costs .25 cents to make them and you sell them for a $1. Your net is .75 cents. if you want to make $1,500 per month you divide $1,500 into .75 and that will tell you that you need to sell 2,000 brownies per month. This is also how you are going to set your goals and this will help you to stay on track.

Cost of your product/service: _____

Price you are selling your product/service: _____

Net Profit: _____

Monthly income goal: _____

Divide your net profit into your monthly goal   _____

This represents how many products/services you need to sell each month.

Estimate Start-up Costs

This can be a difficult conversation to have. So I really need you to pay attention and make good notes. If you miss the boat on this one you can cause yourself a lot of financial problems. When we talk of start up costs, you want to know exactly how much money you need to buy everything you need in order to start your business. This could mean that you have equipment to buy or if you need to rent a retail location or warehouse. I would encourage you to really be conservative here. Only put down the items or things you need to start up your business. Make sure you include paying an employee or even yourself. You really need to keep it real. If there is something you are worried about having to buy later or you are not sure if you will need it, add it to your figures.

I want to help you brain storm and write down a list of items that are common in starting a business. I then want you to make your own list. Don't worry about costs at this time. Once you write down all the items you need then you can go back and write down costs.

Items that might be needed in starting a business:

Office supplies (paper, writing utensils, and calendar)

Office equipment (computer, desk, chair, lights, dry erase board, phone)

Other equipment – what do you need to make or build your product

Office Space (warehouse, office, retail space)

Creating your business entity (this would include paying attorney fees or costs)

Marketing collateral – brochures, flyers, product price lists

Cost to buy your product or raw materials

Estimating utility bill costs – you still need to pay the light bill

Advertising – this can be very expensive

Licensing – sometimes you need to have a specific license to do business, like a plumber

Insurance – do you need any type of liability or commercial insurance?

This should give you a good start. Make a list below of all your estimated start up costs

Its important to list whether your cost will be an on-going cost or a fixed cost or if the cost does not occur frequently this would be a variable cost. Describe the cost below, write down the cost next to it and list it as a fixed cost or a variable cost. This will help you to establish your budget so you can keep track of when your costs are going to come out of your bank account.

Description Cost

_____

_____

_____

_____

_____

_____

_____

_____

_____

_____

_____

_____

_____

_____

_____

_____

_____

_____

_____

_____

STEP SIX

Marketing – Your Plan of Attack

We talked about before how you are going to do free marketing at first and then we can go after the other people that we don't know.

In order to do this we need to know what to say. A Unique Selling Proposition is a simple paragraph that you will want to memorize and tell someone in about 20 seconds. This will help you indentify immediately if the person you are speaking to is interested in what you are selling.

How to create a USP or a unique selling proposition.

When you first meet people they don't care about the name of your company. They only care about what you do. If they like what you do then you can tell them the name of your company

To create your USP, Write down at least 5 things that you do or sell. Be specific. For example, you sell brownies, but they are glutin free brownies. You may write down

1. you sell brownies,

2. they are glutin free,

3. healthy,

4. low calorie and

5. they have healthy chocolate in them.

This can take some time to figure out what is best to say. I like to start by writing down as many items about my business as I can. These items are going to be specific about your product or service. Telling someone that you have superior customer service is not something that has anything to do with your product. Be product/service specific.

Here is an example of what your USP may sound like,

> "we are the company that sells gluten free brownies that are made with healthy chocolate so they are low calorie and good for you.

Feel free to use the context of this example and fill in the appropriate specifics for your business.

Write all the items about your product that others would want to know.

Make your list here:

_____

_____

_____

_____

_____

_____

_____

_____

_____

_____

_____

_____

You should have a pretty good idea of what to say to your potential customers.

Next I want you to identify to whom you want to deliver this USP?

_____

Who is your ideal customer?

_____

Do you want to sell your product/service to Businesses or Directly to Consumers?

_____

Don't be afraid to be very specific. Example: If you are selling to Businesses, what size of company are you looking for? How many employees do they have? Is there an industry that you want to target? Maybe you only want to sell to a specific geographic area,

If you want to sell directly to the consumer. Are they male or female? How much money do they make? Where do they live? What are their hobbies? What do they do in their spare time? How many kids do they have? Do they have any animals?

I think you get the idea.

Now I want you to focus on what is better about what you are selling. We call this the competitive advantage?

What are you doing that your competition is not doing

What specific need are you filling?

Use the info from the previous step to figure out where your customers are located.

Example: maybe you selling an organic baby lotion and you want to sell to those that raise their kids with organic food and use cloth diapers. You find on the internet there is a blog that has mommies that talk about using cloth diapers

Make some notes below:

_____

_____

_____

_____

_____

_____

_____

_____

_____

_____

_____

_____

_____

_____

_____

_____

_____

_____

_____

_____

Company Structure

Depending on how serious you are going to get about your business you need to think about protecting yourself and your business from customers, your competition and any economic conditions that may arise.

This is the part that I take a step back. I could get in trouble for advising you on what entity is the best for you. I would suggest talking to an accountant or corporate attorney. We all seem to have a friend or know someone that is an accountant or attorney. Most of the time it is a simple conversation. I am going to list out the various entities so you know what they are and so you can make a educated decision when you talk with one of these professionals.

Listed below are various business entities or types of business structures you can start.

Sole Proprietor - A **sole proprietorship**, also known as the **sole trader** or simply a **proprietorship**, is a type of business entity that is owned and run by one individual and in which there is no legal distinction between the owner and the business.

The owner receives all profits (subject to taxation specific to the business) and has unlimited responsibility for all losses and debts. Every asset of the business is owned by the proprietor and all debts of the business are the proprietor's. It is a "sole" proprietorship in contrast with partnerships. A sole proprietor may use a trade name or business name other than his or her legal name.

Advantages

- It is easy to organize and needs only small amounts of capital to start and run.
- It permits a high degree of flexibility for the owner since he/she is the boss of the business establishment.
- Due to the owner's unlimited liability, some creditors are more willing to extend credit.
- The owner receives all the profit of the business.
- There is secrecy in sole proprietorship.

Disadvantages

Raising capital for a proprietorship is more difficult because an unrelated investor has less peace of mind concerning the use and security of his or her investment and the investment is more difficult to formalize;[1] other types of business entities have more documentation. The enterprise may be crippled or terminated if the owner becomes ill. Since the business is the same legal entity as the proprietor, it ceases to exist upon the proprietor's death. Because the enterprise rests exclusively on one person, it often has difficulty raising long-term capital.

- Has limited resources. Banks are reluctant to grant loans to single proprietorship considering its small assets and high mortality rate.
- Unlimited liability for business debts. The single owner is responsible for paying all debts and damages of their business.
- If the firm fails, creditors may force the sale of the proprietor's personal property as well as their business property to satisfy their claim.

- When the owner dies, the continuation of the business is difficult, because a new owner must typically accept all liabilities of the business

Limited Liability Corporation - A Limited Liability Company (LLC) is a hybrid business entity having certain characteristics of both a corporation and a partnership or sole proprietorship (depending on how many owners there are). An LLC, although a business entity, is a type of unincorporated association and is not a corporation. The primary characteristic an LLC shares with a corporation is limited liability, and the primary characteristic it shares with a partnership is the availability of pass-through income taxation. It is often more flexible than a corporation, and it is well-suited for companies with a single owner.

LLC members are subject to the same alter ego piercing theories as corporate shareholders. However, it is more difficult to pierce the LLC veil because LLCs do not have many formalities to maintain. So long as the LLC and the members do not commingle funds, it would be difficult to pierce its veil. Membership interests in LLCs and partnership interests are also afforded a significant level of protection through the charging order mechanism. The charging order limits the creditor of a debtor-partner or a debtor-member to the debtor's share of distributions, without conferring on the creditor any voting or management rights. Limited liability company members may, in certain circumstances, also incur a personal liability in cases where distributions to members render the LLC insolvent.

Advantages

- Choice of tax regime. An LLC can elect to be taxed as a sole proprietor, partnership, S corporation or C corporation (as long as they would otherwise qualify for such tax treatment), providing for a great deal of flexibility.

- A limited liability company with multiple members that elects to be taxed as partnership may specially allocate the members' distributive share of income, gain, loss, deduction, or credit via the company operating agreement on a basis other than the ownership percentage of each member so long as the rules contained in Treasury Regulation (26 CFR) 1.704-1 are met. S corporations may not specially allocate profits, losses and other tax items under US tax law.

- Limited liability, meaning that the owners of the LLC, called "members", are protected from some or all liability for acts and debts of the LLC depending on state shield laws.

- Much less administrative paperwork and record keeping than a corporation.

- Pass-through taxation (i.e., no double taxation), unless the LLC elects to be taxed as a C corporation.

- Using default tax classification, profits are taxed personally at the member level, not at the LLC level.

- LLCs in most states are treated as entities separate from their members.

- LLCs in some states can be set up with just one natural person involved.

- Less risk to be "stolen" by fire-sale acquisitions (more protection against "hungry" investors).

- For real estate companies, each separate property can be owned by its own, individual LLC, thereby shielding not only the owners, but their other properties from cross-liability.

Disadvantages

Although there is no statutory requirement for an operating agreement in most jurisdictions, members of a multiple member LLC who operate without one may run into problems. Unlike state laws regarding stock corporations, which are very well developed and provide for a variety of governance and protective provisions for the corporation and its shareholders, most states do not dictate detailed governance and protective provisions for the members of a limited liability company. Thus, in the absence of such statutory provisions, the members of an LLC must establish governance and protective provisions pursuant to an operating agreement or similar governing document.

- It may be more difficult to raise financial capital for an LLC as investors may be more comfortable investing funds in the better-understood corporate form with a view toward an eventual IPO. One possible solution may be to form a new corporation and merge into it, dissolving the LLC and converting into a corporation.

- The management structure of an LLC may be unfamiliar to many. Unlike corporations, they are not required to have a board of directors or officers. (This could also be seen as an advantage to some.)

- Taxing jurisdictions outside the US are likely to treat a US LLC as a corporation, regardless of its treatment for US tax purposes, for example if a US LLC does business outside the US or a resident of a foreign jurisdiction is a member of a US LLC.

- The principals of LLCs use many different titles—e.g., member, manager, managing member, managing director, chief executive officer, president, and partner. As such, it can be difficult to determine who actually has the authority to enter into a contract on the LLC's behalf.

S Corporation - S corporations are merely corporations that elect to pass corporate income, losses, deductions, and credit through to their shareholders for federal tax purposes. The S corporation rules are contained in Subchapter S of Chapter 1 of the Internal Revenue Code (sections 1361 through 1379). S status combines the legal environment of C corporations with U.S. federal income taxation similar to that of partnerships.

Like a C corporation, an S corporation is generally a corporation under the law of the state in which the entity is organized. For Federal income tax purposes, however, taxation of S corporations resembles that of partnerships. As with partnerships, the income, deductions, and tax credits of an S corporation flow through to shareholders annually, regardless of whether distributions are made. Thus, income is taxed at the shareholder level and not at the corporate level. Payments to S shareholders by the corporation are distributed tax-free to the extent that the distributed earnings were previously taxed. Also, certain corporate penalty taxes (e.g., accumulated earnings tax, personal holding company tax) and the alternative minimum tax do not apply to an S corporation.

Unlike a C corporation, an S corporation is not eligible for a dividends received deduction.

Unlike a C corporation, an S corporation is not subject to the 10 percent of taxable income limitation applicable to charitable contribution deductions.

Qualification for S corporation status

In order to make an election to be treated as an S corporation, the following requirements must be met:

- Must be an eligible entity (a domestic corporation, or a limited liability company which has elected to be taxed as a corporation).
- Must have only one class of stock.
- Must not have more than 100 shareholders.

- Spouses are automatically treated as a single shareholder. Families, defined as individuals descended from a common ancestor, plus spouses and former spouses of either the common ancestor or anyone lineally descended from that person, are considered a single shareholder as long as any family member elects such treatment.[2]

- Shareholders must be U.S. citizens or residents, and must be natural persons, so corporate shareholders and partnerships are generally excluded. However, certain trusts, estates, and tax-exempt corporations, notably 501(c)(3)corporations, are permitted to be shareholders.

- Profits and losses must be allocated to shareholders proportionately to each one's interest in the business.

If a corporation meets the foregoing requirements and wishes to be taxed under Subchapter S, its shareholders may file Form 2553: "Election by a Small Business Corporation" with the Internal Revenue Service (IRS). The Form 2553 must be signed by all of the corporation's shareholders. If a shareholder resides in a community property state, the shareholder's spouse generally must also sign the 2553.

The S corporation election must typically be made by the fifteenth day of the third month of the tax year for which the election is intended to be effective, or at any time during the year immediately preceding the tax year.Congress has directed the IRS to show leniency with regard to late S elections. Accordingly, often, the IRS will accept a late S election.

Some states such as New York and New Jersey require a separate state-level S election in order for the corporation to be treated, for state tax purposes, as an S corporation.

If a corporation that has elected to be treated as an S corporation ceases to meet the requirements (for example, if as a result of stock transfers, the number of shareholders exceeds 100 or an ineligible shareholder such as a nonresident alien acquires a share), the corporation will lose its S corporation status and revert to being a regular C corporation.

If more than 25% of a S-corporation's gross receipts consists of passive income for three consecutive years when the corporation has accumulated earnings and profits, the S corporation will automatically lose its subchapter S status and revert to being a regular C corporation.

C Corporation - In the United States, corporations are formed under laws of a state or the District of Columbia. Procedures vary widely by state. Some states allow formation of corporations through electronic filing on the state's web site or very quickly. All states require payment of a fee (often under USD200) upon incorporation.[4] Corporations are issued a "certificate of incorporation" by most states upon formation. Most state corporate laws require that the basic governing instrument be either the certificate of incorporation or formal articles of incorporation. Many corporations also adopt additional governing rules known as bylaws. Most state laws require at least one director and at least two officers, all of whom may be the same person. Generally there are no residency requirements for officers or directors.

Financial statements

Corporations are required to issue financial statements in the United States. Financial statements may be presented on any comprehensive basis, including an income tax basis. There is no requirement for appointment of auditors, unless the corporation is publicly traded and thus subject to the requirements of the Sarbanes-Oxley Act.

Distributions

Any distribution from the earnings and profits of a C corporation is treated as a dividend for U.S. income tax purposes. "Earnings and profits" is a tax law concept similar to the financial accounting concept of retained earnings. Exceptions apply to treat certain distributions as made in exchange for stock rather than as dividends. Such exceptions include distributions in complete termination of a shareholder's interest and distributions in liquidation of the corporation

Non for Profit Company – also known colloquially as either a **501(c)** or a "**nonprofit**", is an American tax-exempt nonprofit organization. Section 501(c) of the United States Internal Revenue Code (26 U.S.C. § 501(c)) provides that 29 types of nonprofit organizations are exempt from some federal income taxes. Sections 503 through 505 set out the requirements for attaining such exemptions. Many states refer to Section 501(c) for definitions of organizations exempt from state taxation as well.

The basic requirement of getting tax exempt status is that the organization is specifically limited in powers to purposes that the IRS classifies as tax exempt purposes. Unlike for-profit corporations that benefit from broad and general purposes, nonprofit organizations need to be limited in powers to function with tax exempt status, but a nonprofit corporation is by default not limited in powers until it specifically limits itself in the articles of incorporation and/or nonprofit corporate bylaws. This limiting of the powers is crucial to obtaining tax exempt status with the IRS and then on the state level

Where to get the money you need for your business

You may know or have already experienced getting money to start a business can be pretty difficult. Some of us are fortunate because we may know a family member or a close friend with deep pockets, but for the rest of us it is scraping every penny we got to make it all work.

So what are the traditional means to get money? Well you have the bank loan. In order to get a loan you need to have really good credit and collateral. Collateral means that you have something of value to give up if you cannot pay your loan back. Another method is going after an Angel investor or venture capital. This can be very difficult but very rewarding if you get picked up by one. Angels and venture capital (VC) companies are businesses that lend out their money for part of your company. I have found that the companies that get picked up by Angels and VC's are tech savvy companies.

Of course there is always the credit card route. I have known many to apply for 5-10 credit cards all at the same time and us them to fund their business. I want you to know that I am not recommending this route, but I have seen many do it.... Including myself.

I don't know if you have heard of this yet, it seems to be getting pretty popular. It is called crowd funding. Crowd funding is pretty simple to understand. It is basically getting people to contribute small amounts of money to your project and there is no payback. The hard part is making your new opportunity sound so awesome that people want to give you money. You can search the internet to find the best crowd funding website.

Start getting the word out

Use your contact list you made earlier and start calling, emailing, texting and talking to people about your new business. This should be a really exciting time for you. Go shout it to all that you know.

I also recommend to people to start a face book page or a twitter account. These are powerful tools to get all those who like your business to be in one place. This helps you to tell your "peeps" about the entire cool stuff your doing or tell them about special deals. It also allows your "peeps" to make positive comments about your business so others will get excited also. I also like these two social medias because it helps you keep your face and name in front of them. If you want to create loyal customers you need to let them know you are there for them.

You may want to consider doing a blog. Some people like to do this because it allows you to tell stories and give meaning to the products or services that you are providing.

Glossary

Asset - Anything tangible or intangible that is capable of being owned or controlled to produce value and that is held to have positive economic value

Balance - is the amount of money owed, (or due), that remains in a deposit account (or a loan account) at a given date, after all past remittances, payments and withdrawal have been accounted for. It can be positive (then, in the balance sheet of a firm, it is an asset) or negative (a liability).

Balloon Payment – a loan which does not fully amortize over the term of the note, thus leaving a balance due at maturity. The final payment is called a *balloon payment* because of its large size. Balloon payment loans are more common in commercial real estate. The loan may have a fixed or a floating interest rate.

Bankrupt - a legal status of a person or other entity that cannot repay the debts it owes to creditors. In most jurisdictions, bankruptcy is imposed by a court order, often initiated by the debtor.

Board of advisors - a body that advises the management of a corporation, organization, or foundation. Unlike the Board of Directors the advisory board does not have authority to vote on corporate matters, nor a legal fiduciary responsibility. Many new or small businesses choose to have advisory boards in order to benefit from the knowledge of others, without the expense or formality of the Board of Directors.

Brand - is the "name, term, design, symbol, or any other feature that identifies one seller's product distinct from those of other sellers

Business - is an organization involved in the trade of goods, services, or both to consumers. Businesses are predominant in capitalist economies, where most of them are privately owned and administered to provide service to customers for profit.

Capital - capital consists of any produced thing that can enhance a person's power to perform economically useful work

Cash flow - is the movement of money into or out of a business, project, or financial product. It is usually measured during a specified, limited period of time. Measurement of cash flow can be used for calculating other parameters that give information on a company's value and situation.

Competitive Advantage - when an organization acquires or develops an attribute or combination of attributes that allows it to outperform its competitors.

Corporation – is a separate legal entity that has been incorporated through a legislative or registration process established through legislation. Incorporated entities have legal rights and liabilities that are

74

distinct from their employees and shareholders,[1] and may conduct business as either a profit-seeking business or not for profit business

Credit - is the trust which allows one party to provide resources to another party. a representation of credit worthiness. Type of bookkeeping entry that leads to a positive to an account

Debit - Type of bookkeeping entry that leads to a negative to an account

Demand - is an economic principle that describes a consumer's desire, willingness and ability to pay a price for a specific good or service. Demand refers to how much (quantity) of a product or service is desired by buyers.

Due Diligence - is a term used for a number of concepts, involving either an investigation of a business or person prior to signing a contract, or an act with a certain standard of care.

Factoring - is a financial transaction in which a business sells its accounts receivable (i.e., invoices) to a third party (called a factor) at a discount

Finance - is the science of funds management, or the allocation of assets and liabilities over time under conditions of certainty and uncertainty. A key point in finance is the time value of money, which states that a unit of currency today is worth more than the same unit of currency tomorrow.

Gross Profit - or **sales profit** is the difference between revenue and the cost of making a product or providing a service, before deducting overhead, payroll, taxation, and interest payments

Income - is the sum of all the wages, salaries, profits, interests payments, rents and other forms of earnings received... in a given period of time

Leverage - is a general term for any technique to multiply gains and losses. Leverage exists when an investor achieves the right to a return on a capital base that exceeds the investment which the investor has personally contributed to the entity or instrument achieving a return. Common ways to attain leverage are borrowing money, buying fixed assets and using derivatives

Liable - a person is legally liable when they are financially and legally responsible for something

Liability - can mean something that is a hindrance or puts an individual or group at a disadvantage, or something that someone is responsible for, or something that increases the chance of something occurring (i.e. it is a cause). a current obligation of an entity arising from past transactions or events

Limited liability Corporation (LLC) - is a flexible form of enterprise that blends elements of partnership and corporate structures. An LLC is not a corporation; it is a legal form of company that provides limited liability to its owners in the vast majority of United States jurisdictions. LLCs do not need to be organized for profit

Management - in all business and organizational activities is the act of coordinating the efforts of people to accomplish desired goals and objectives using available resources efficiently and effectively. Management comprises planning, organizing, staffing, leading or directing, and controlling an organization (a group of one or more people or entities) or effort for the purpose of accomplishing a goal.

Mentor - relationship in which a more experienced or more knowledgeable person helps to guide a less experienced or less knowledgeable person. However, true mentoring is more than just answering occasional questions or providing ad hoc help. It is about an ongoing relationship of learning, dialogue, and challenge.

Middleman - is a third party that offers *intermediation* services between two trading parties. The *intermediary* acts as a conduit for goods or services offered by a supplier to a consumer

Networking - is a socioeconomic activity by which groups of like-minded businesspeople recognize, create, or act upon business opportunities. A business network is a type of social network whose reason for existing is business activity

Net - the sum or difference of two or more variables (as in net worth). The opposite of gross.

Outsourcing - is the contracting out of a business process to a third-party.

Overhead - the ongoing operating costs of running a business

Patent - is a set of exclusive rights granted by a sovereign state to an inventor or their assignee for a limited period of time, in exchange for the public disclosure of the invention. An invention is a solution to a specific technological problem, and may be a product or a process. Patents are a form of intellectual property.

Principle - is a law or rule. Can be a majority shareholder(s) in a company or corporation

Product - an item that ideally satisfies a market's want or need

Profit - the difference between the purchase price and the costs of bringing to market

Promissory note - is a legal instrument (more particularly, a financial instrument), in which one party (the *maker* or *issuer*) promises in writing to pay a determinate sum of money to the other (the *payee*), either at a fixed or determinable future time or on demand of the payee, under specific terms. If the promissory note is unconditional and readily salable, it is called a negotiable instrument.

Public domain - are those whose intellectual property rights have expired, have been forfeited, or are inapplicable.

Rate of return - also known as **return on investment (ROI)**, **rate of profit** or sometimes just **return**, is the ratio of money gained or lost (whether realized or unrealized) on an investment relative to the amount of money invested.

Revenue - is income that a company receives from its normal business activities, usually from the sale of goods and services to customers.

Risk - is the potential of loss (an undesirable outcome, however not necessarily so) resulting from a given action, activity and/or inaction

Royalty - the payment made (originally to the licensing crown) for a concession of commercial value (e.g. mining rights) or to the owner of a copyright, patent, trademark or know-how for its use

Sales tax - is a tax paid to a governing body for the sales of certain goods and services. Usually laws allow (or require) the seller to collect funds for the tax from the consumer at the point of purchase.

Saving account - are accounts maintained by retail financial institutions that pay interest but cannot be used directly as money in the narrow sense of a medium of exchange (for example, by writing a check). These accounts let customers set aside a portion of their liquid assets while earning a monetary return.

Service - the non-material equivalent of a good in economics and marketing, within the service-product continuum

Sole proprietor - also known as the **sole trader** or simply a **proprietorship**, is a type of business entity that is owned and run by one individual and in which there is no legal distinction between the owner and the business.

Start-up costs – The money required to buy the necessary products, materials, goods to start a business in which the goal is to make money or function as a not profit. This could also include wages and salaries to those you have hired to run your business

Supply - the amount of a product which is available to customers

Tax - is a financial charge or other levy imposed upon a taxpayer (an individual or legal entity) by a state or the functional equivalent of a state such that failure to pay is punishable by law.

Tax exemption - may provide a potential taxpayer complete relief from tax, tax at a reduced rate, or tax on only a portion of the items subject to tax. Examples include exemption of charitable
organizations from property taxes and income taxes, exemptions provided to veterans, and exemptions under cross-border or multi-jurisdictional principles.

Tax evasion - is the illegal evasion of taxes by
individuals, corporations and trusts. Tax evasion often entails taxpayers deliberately misrepresenting the true state of their affairs to the tax authorities to reduce their tax liability and includes dishonest tax

reporting, such as declaring less income, profits or gains than the amounts actually earned, or overstating deductions

Trademark - is a recognizable sign, design or expression which identifies products or services of a particular source from those of others

Unique selling proposition - (USP), or unique selling point, is a marketing concept first proposed as a theory to explain a pattern in successful advertising campaigns of the early 1940s. The USP states that such campaigns made unique propositions to the customer that convinced them to switch brands. The term was developed by television advertising pioneer Rosser Reeves of Ted Bates & Company. Theodore Levitt, a professor at Harvard Business School, suggested that, "Differentiation is one of the most important strategic and tactical activities in which companies must constantly engage."The term has been used to describe one's "personal brand" in the marketplace. Today, the term is used in other fields or just casually to refer to any aspect of an object that differentiates it from similar objects.

Working capital - is a financial metric which represents operating liquidity available to a business, organization or other entity, including governmental entity. Along with fixed assets such as plant and equipment, working capital is considered a part of operating capital.

RESOURCES

Small Business Administration (sba.gov)

409 3rd St SW, Washington DC 20416

800-827-5722

SCORE (score.org)

26 Federal Plaza, New York City, NY 10021

212-264-4507

National Association of Women Business Owners

1413 K St NW #637, Washington DC 20003

301-608-2590

Trademark/Patent Service

E-Trademark Universe

Tel: (505) 999-1498

Fax: (505) 832-3377

info@e-trademarkuniverse.com

www.linkedin.com/in/etrademarkuniverse

www.ingramcontent.com/pod-product-compliance
Lightning Source LLC
Chambersburg PA
CBHW081836170526
45167CB00007B/2824